Bunny Island

Pippa Kennard

Photography by
Yukihiro Fukuda

FIREFLY BOOKS

Welcome to bunny island. We have busy days filled with all sorts of fun.

Come meet my friends!

I'm just waking up. Good morning!

Look at me run!
Bunnies are quick.

ZOOM

ZOOM

ZOOM

Who can jump the highest?

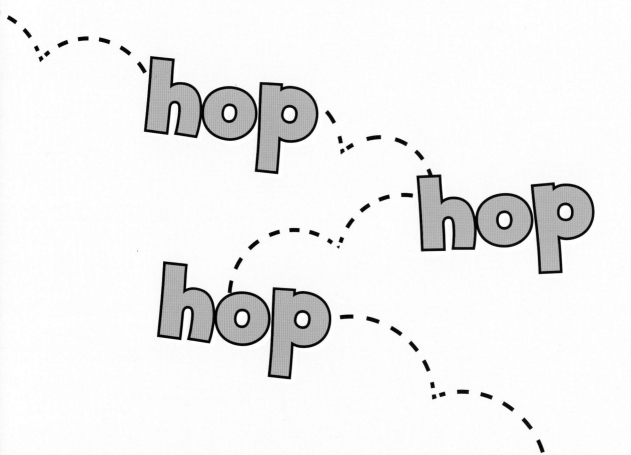

Did you know that bunnies like to make holes?

dig

dig

dig

I just went for a swim.
Where's my towel?

My friend and I are always telling jokes.

Wiggle

Wiggle

My mom makes me eat leafy greens too!

munch

munch munch

munch

I am one thirsty bunny!

slurp

slurp

slurp

Mom always gives me a goodnight kiss!

Now it's time for bed, sleepyhead.

zzz

zzz

zzz

I hope you had fun! Now it's time for me to go to bed.

Dedication
For Ashley, with love.

Acknowledgments
**Special thanks to Michael Worek,
Allison Pries and Lauren Booth.**

Published by Firefly Books Ltd. 2015
Copyright © 2015 Firefly Books Ltd.
Text copyright © 2015 Pippa Kennard
Photographs copyright © 2015 Yukihiro Fukuda

First printing

Publisher Cataloging-in-Publication Data (U.S.)
Kennard, Pippa.
Bunny Island / Pippa Kennard ; photography by Yukihiro Fukuda.
[32] pages : color photographs ; cm.
Summary: "In the Sea of Japan lies Okunoshima Island, a popular wildlife tourist destination that is teeming with wild bunnies. These adorable creatures are captured in full-color full-page photography. The bunnies' antics are accentuated with a repetitive text to teach young children action words." – Provided by publisher.
ISBN-13: 978-1-77085-658-5
ISBN-13: 978-1-77085-657-8 (pbk.)
1. Rabbits – Juvenile literature.   I. Title. 2. Fukuda, Yukihiro.
599.32 dc23   QL737.L32K466 2015

Library and Archives Canada Cataloguing in Publication
Kennard, Pippa, author
Bunny Island / Pippa Kennard ; photography by Yukihiro Fukuda.
ISBN 978-1-77085-658-5 (bound).--ISBN 978-1-77085-657-8 (pbk.)
1. Rabbits--Juvenile literature. 2. Islands--Japan--Hiroshima ken--Juvenile literature. 3. Vocabulary--Juvenile literature. I. Fukuda, Yukihiro, 1965-, photographer II. Title.
QL737.L32K46 2015   j599.32   C2015-903108-7

Published in the United States by
Firefly Books (U.S.) Inc.
P.O. Box 1338, Ellicott Station
Buffalo, New York 14205

Published in Canada by
Firefly Books Ltd.
50 Staples Avenue, Unit 1
Richmond Hill, Ontario L4B 0A7

Cover and interior design: Hartley Millson

Printed in China

The publisher gratefully acknowledges the financial support for our publishing program by the Government of Canada through the Canada Book Fund as administered by the Department of Canadian Heritage.